PLANET

EARTH

By Rosie Rowntree

CONTENTS

First published in 2026 by Hungry Tomato Ltd
F15, Old Bakery Studios, Blewetts Wharf, Malpas Road,
Truro, Cornwall, TR1 1QH, UK.

 A CIP catalog record for this book is available from the British Library.

ISBN 9781835696774

Manufactured in the USA

Discover more at
www.hungrytomato.com

Front cover image is an edited image of Earth and the International Space Station. Title page image is an edited image of Earth. Contents page image is an edited image of Earth.

Words in **BOLD** can be found in the glossary.

WHERE IS EARTH?

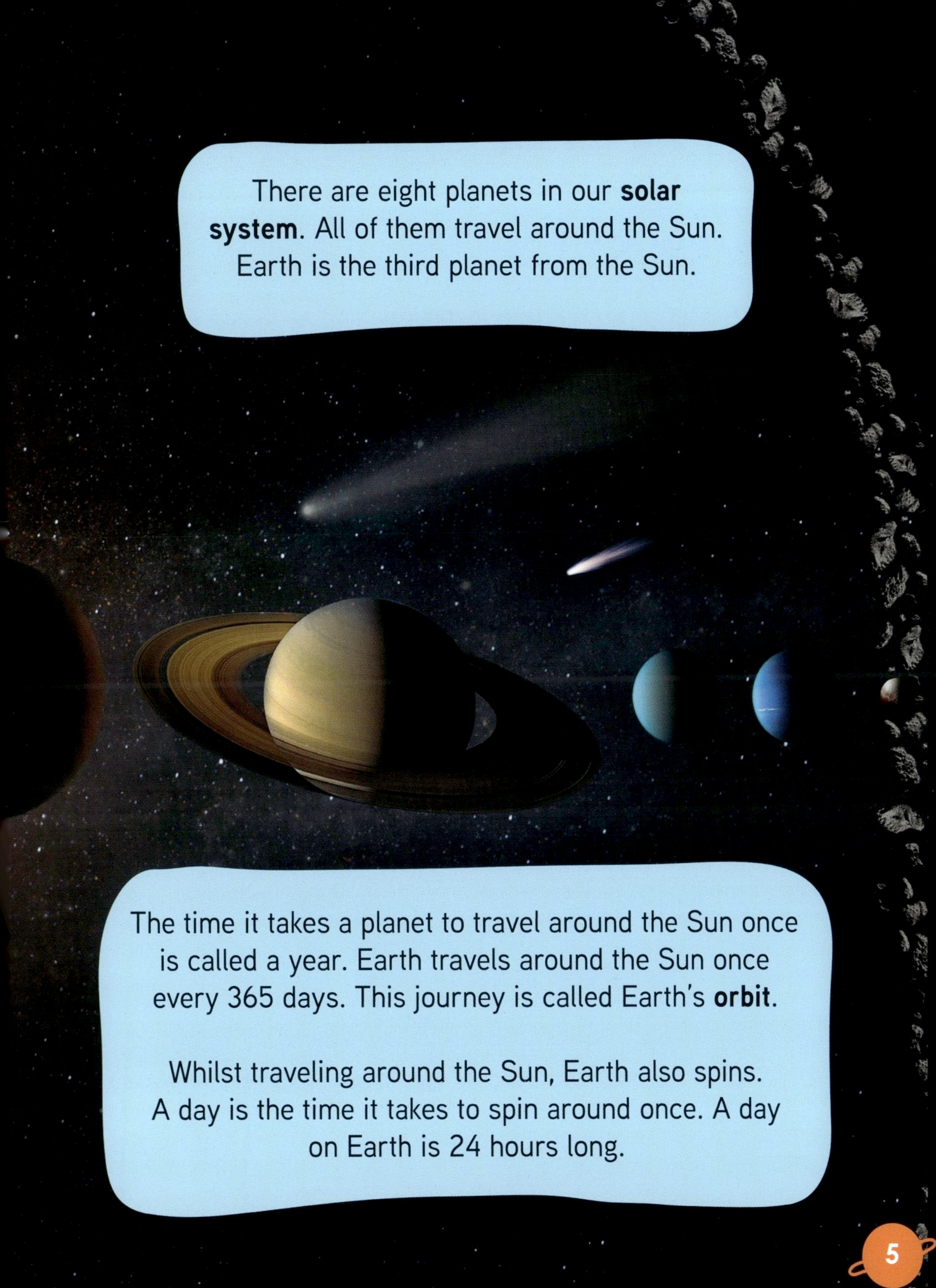

There are eight planets in our **solar system**. All of them travel around the Sun. Earth is the third planet from the Sun.

The time it takes a planet to travel around the Sun once is called a year. Earth travels around the Sun once every 365 days. This journey is called Earth's **orbit**.

Whilst traveling around the Sun, Earth also spins. A day is the time it takes to spin around once. A day on Earth is 24 hours long.

PLANET FACTS

Earth is the only planet in our solar system that has liquid water on its surface. It's what makes life possible!

Water covers most of Earth's surface. It is one of the most precious things on our planet, and we must look after it!

The Great Barrier Reef is the largest living structure on Earth. It, and all **ecosystems** in our ocean, are very important to life because they produce most of the **oxygen** that we need to breathe!

WHAT'S THE WEATHER LIKE?

The weather on Earth is always changing because the air in the **atmosphere** is always moving.

It can be freezing in one place, and boiling hot in another! But most of Earth is neither too hot nor too cold – perfect for life!

The record for the highest temperature on Earth was set in Death Valley in the United States. It reached 135.8 °F (57.7 °C)!

32 °F (0 °C) is the temperature that water freezes at.

The coldest place on Earth is Antarctica. The temperature once went down all the way to -135 °F (-93 °C)!

CHANGING TEMPERATURES

When things like oil and coal are burned, a **gas** called **carbon dioxide** is created.

Carbon dioxide gets trapped in the atmosphere and stops heat from escaping. This causes temperatures on Earth to rise.

Something similar has already happened on Venus, which is now too hot and dry for life to survive!

EARTH'S CRUST

Earth is made of different layers. The outer layer, that we all live on, is called the crust.

Earth's crust is split into sections called **tectonic plates** that all fit together like a giant jigsaw puzzle!

These plates are always slowly moving. If they move suddenly, the ground can start to shake! We call this an **earthquake**.

Inner core

The middle of Earth is split into two sections called the inner and outer **core**. The inner core is as hot as the Sun!

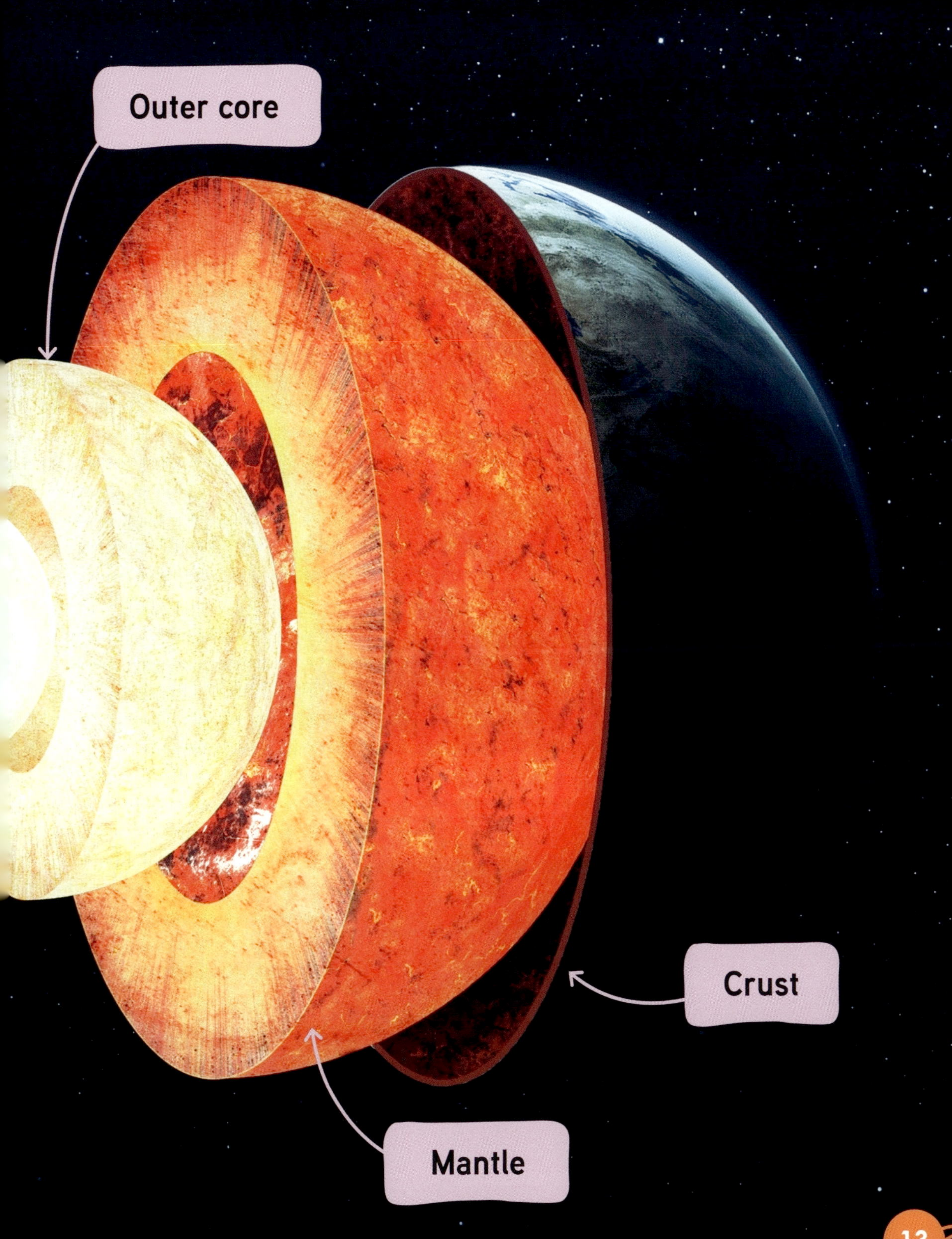
Outer core
Crust
Mantle

ON THE SURFACE

The plates that make up Earth's crust also create the **mountains** that cover our planet's surface.

Over millions of years, two plates pushing against each other can start pushing layers of rock upwards to make mountains.

Sometimes, when Earth's plates move, it can create a crack in the crust. This allows **molten** rock to bubble through and create volcanoes!

Mount Everest is the tallest mountain on Earth. It is so tall that its **peak** is sometimes higher than the clouds!

FACT FILE

An invisible force called **gravity** keeps our feet on the ground and stops us from drifting away into space! Gravity is also what keeps Earth orbiting the Sun, and the Moon orbiting Earth.

The Moon is Earth's only **satellite**. Apart from the Sun, it is the brightest thing that we can see in the sky. Earth is the only planet in the solar system with just one moon!

The biggest ocean on Earth is the Pacific Ocean. It's over five times wider than the Moon is!

EXPLORING EARTH

Earth is the only planet we know of that has life on it! Humans, animals, and plants of all shapes and sizes live all across our planet.

Animals like the snow leopard live at incredibly high **altitudes** on the sides of mountains.

Snow leopard

Certain kinds of whales can hold their breath for several hours and can dive very far underwater. The bottom of Earth's oceans are so deep that sunlight can't reach – it's completely black down there!

HUMANS IN SPACE

Humans have always loved exploring – that includes exploring outer space too! People who travel into space are called **astronauts**.

Astronauts get to space by launching on top of powerful rockets.

Many of them live onboard **space stations** for months before returning to Earth.

While in space, they conduct scientific experiments that help us to learn more about our planet!

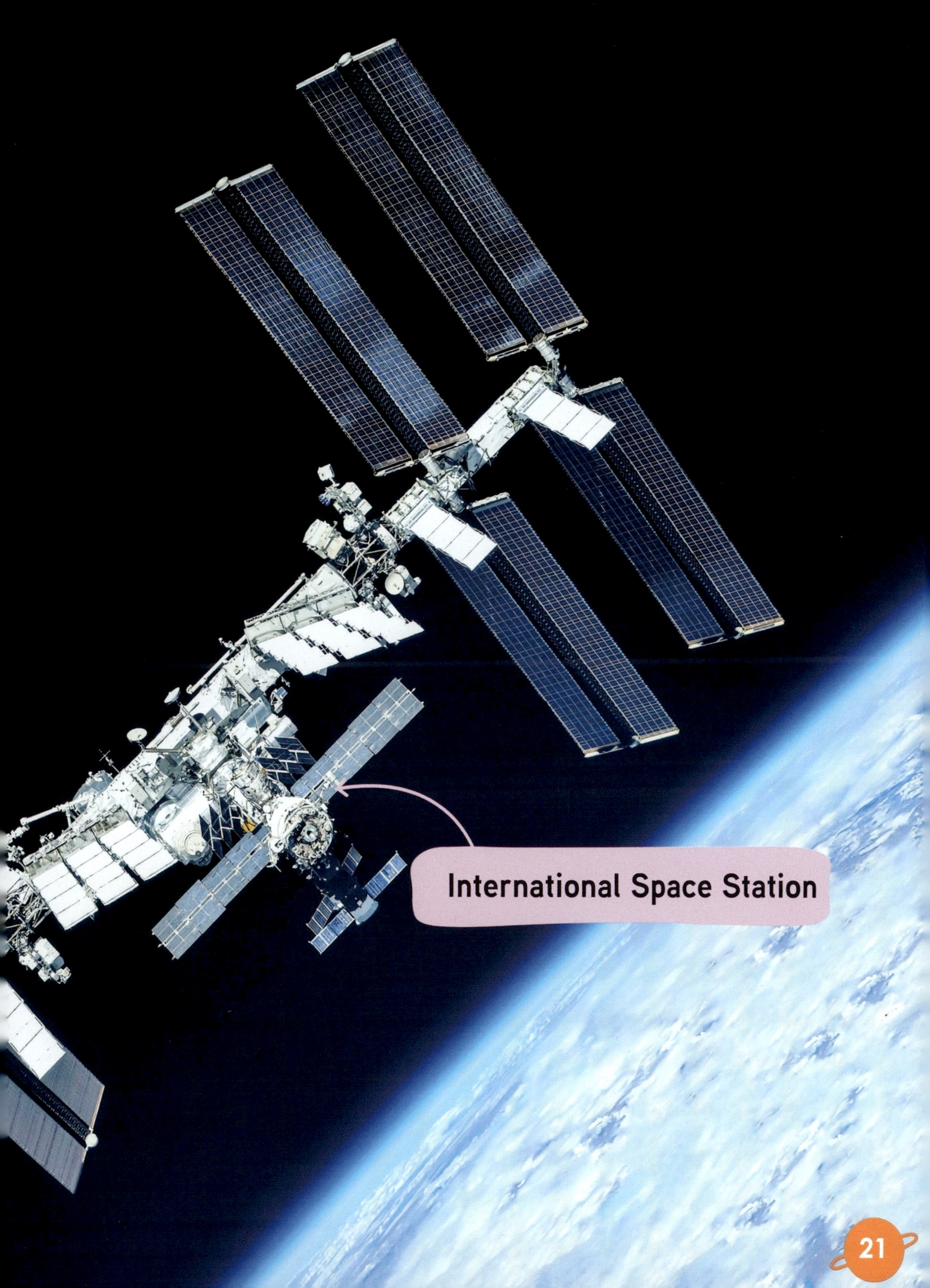
International Space Station

WHAT'S NEXT?

There is still so much to learn about Earth. Scientists use things like satellites and **robots** to find out more about Earth, and do things that it would be hard for humans to do.

Satellites up in space can take photographs of huge areas of land below. These can be used to make detailed maps!

Satellite

Robots can explore the oceans, far deeper than humans are able to swim. They have found lots of unusual-looking animals that live in the depths!

GLOSSARY

Altitude – the height of something above Earth's surface.

Astronauts – people trained to travel into outer space.

Atmosphere – the gases that surround a planet.

Carbon dioxide – an invisible gas in the air.

Core – the middle of a planet.

Earthquake – when parts of the ground shake. Earthquake can be very strong and destructive.

Ecosystems – all the living and non-living things that exist together within an area.

Gas – a substance that is neither solid nor liquid, and has no fixed shape. Many gases are invisible.

Gravity – an invisible force that pulls things together. Gravity keeps our feet on the ground and the planets spinning around the Sun.

Molten – another word for melted.

Mountains – rocky landforms that rise high above their surroundings.

Orbit – the path taken by one object circling around another in space.

Oxygen – an invisible gas in the air that people and animals need to breathe.

Peak – the very top of a mountain.

Robots – machines controlled by a computer that can do tasks on their own without a human.

Satellite – things that orbit around a planet. They can be natural, like the Moon, or human-made.

Solar system – the Sun and everything that moves around it.

Space stations – large spacecraft in orbit around Earth where astronauts live.

Tectonic platers – huge pieces of rock that make up the outer layers of Earth.

Picture credits:
(t=top; b=bottom; m=middle; l=left; r=right):

NASA: images-assets.nasa.gov/image/NHQ202210050006/NHQ202210050006~orig.jpg 20ml. Unknown 12mr. Shutterstock: ALHARBII 11tr; Amanda Sala 9tr; Andrea Izzotti 19tl; Andrei Armiagov 22-23bg; Artsiom P 20-21bg; Buradaki 6-7bg; Cynthia A Jackson 7mr; Daniel Prudeck 14-15bg; Diego Grandi 23br; Duranart Wangsuvan 24bg; Florian Nimsdorf 14bl; Holly S Cannon 18mr; Ixpert 1bg; KeyFame 10-11bg; Midnight in Summer 9br; Muratart 16-17bg; Northlight 10mr; Olga_Olechka 9mr; Paula French 16mr; Sergey Nivens 2-3bg; Somavarapu Madhaui 16mr; Triff 4-5bg, 8-9bg; Vadim Sadovski 12-13bg.